THE VERY BEST OF RICHARD DAWKINS

QUOTES FROM A DEVOUT ATHEIST

GORDON FISHER

Copyright © 2014 Gordon Fisher

All rights reserved.

ISBN: 1501066102
ISBN-13: 978-1501066108

CONTENTS

1	Introduction	1
2	About Atheism	3
3	About Himself	5
4	About Other People	13
5	General Opinions	17
6	General Philosophy	25
7	On Religion	33
8	On Science	47

ACKNOWLEDGMENTS

All quotes within this book are in the words of Richard Dawkins. Although every effort has been taken to ensure the accuracy of all text, the author apologises in the event of any mistakes.

1 INTRODUCTION

Richard Dawkins originally made a name for himself as one of the world's leading evolutionary biologists. However, as a 'devout' atheist, he is probably now even better known as one of the most outspoken figures on the negatives of religion in society.

Since his book 'The God Delusion', Dawkins has attracted much attention worldwide from the media. To atheists, he is a voice of reason in an otherwise crazy world; by the religious he has been accused of being patronising and insulting, and even on the fast-track to hell.

Whichever side of the fence you fall on, one has to admire Dawkins for his outspoken views in the face of massive controversy. It takes a brave individual to openly question the beliefs of billions across the planet.

In this book I have collated some of the best and most interesting of Dawkins' quotes in order to give a unique insight into the mind of probably the most famous atheist alive.

2 ABOUT ATHEISM

"Coming out as an atheist can cost an academic his or her job in some parts of America, and many choose to keep quiet about their atheism."

*

"We are all atheists about most of the gods that societies have ever believed in. Some of us just go one god further."

*

"I certainly would absolutely never do what some of my American colleagues do and object to religious symbols being used, putting crosses up in the public square and things like that. I don't fret about that at all; I'm quite happy about that."

*

"Rather than say he's an atheist, a friend of mine says, 'I'm a tooth fairy agnostic,' meaning he can't disprove God but thinks God is about as likely as the tooth fairy."

*

"The universe we observe has precisely the properties we should expect if there is, at bottom, no design, no purpose, no evil, no good, nothing but blind, pitiless indifference."

*

"There are people who try to get atheists to form a sort of atheist church and have atheist community singsongs and things. I don't see the need for that, but if people want to do it, why shouldn't they?"

*

"If children understand that beliefs should be substantiated with evidence, as opposed to tradition, authority, revelation or faith, they will automatically work out for themselves that they are atheists."

3 ABOUT HIMSELF

"There are quite a lot of YouTube clips of me that have gone viral. One that I think of is of a young woman at a lecture I was giving - she came from Liberty University, which is a ludicrous religious institution. She said, 'What if you are wrong?' and I answered that rather briefly, and that's gone viral."

*

"I love words."

*

"If I say that I am more interested in preventing the slaughter of large whales than I am in improving housing conditions for people, I am likely to shock some of my friends."

*

"I did not end up as broadly educated as my Cambridge colleagues, but I graduated probably better equipped to write a book on my chosen subject."

*

"I think looking back to my own childhood, the fact that so many of the stories I read allowed the possibility of frogs turning into princes, whether that has a sort of insidious affect on rationality, I'm not sure. Perhaps it's something for research."

*

"I didn't know children were expected to have literary heroes, but I certainly had one, and I even identified with him at one time: Doctor Dolittle, whom I now half identify with the Charles Darwin of Beagle days."

*

"I don't know what to think about magic and fairy tales."

*

"My decision to be a scientist was a bit of a drift really, more or less by default."

*

"I'm not one of those who wants to purge our society of our Christian history."

*

"In the original introduction to the word meme in the last chapter of 'The Selfish Gene,' I did actually use the metaphor of a 'virus.' So when anybody talks about something going viral on the Internet, that is exactly what a meme is, and it looks as though the word has been appropriated for a subset of that."

*

"I can remember at the age of about six being fascinated by the planets and learning all about Mars and Venus and things."

*

"I like to think 'The God Delusion' is a humorous book. I think, actually, it's full of laughs. And people who describe it as a polarizing book or as an aggressive book, it's just that very often they haven't read it."

*

"My personal feeling is that understanding evolution led me to atheism."

*

"I have begun several projects which were never completed, not necessarily because they failed, but because I got interested in other things."

*

"I was brought up in a family which valued natural history. Both my parents knew the names of all the British wildflowers, so as we went walking the country, I was constantly being exposed to a natural history sort of knowledge."

*

"My interest in biology was pretty much always on the philosophical side."

*

"It doesn't hurt my feelings when I get vilified by fundamentalist religious people. I've actually made comedy out of it. I've made light of that."

*

"I love romantic poetry."

*

"I'm not much given to straight, irony-free hero-worship."

*

"I don't do formal debates, because formal debates where you have two people up on a stage in equal status, and each of them is given 20 minutes to give their point of view, and then 10 minutes for a rebuttal, or whatever, that creates the illusion that you really do have here two equal points of view of equal scientific standing."

*

"I'm not a good observer. I'm not proud of it."

*

"I was never much bothered about moral questions like, 'How could there be a good God when there's so much evil in the world?'"

*

"My thoughts, my beliefs, my feelings are all in my brain. My brain is going to rot."

*

"I can handle heckling on evolution because it's my own field."

*

"I do sometimes accuse people of ignorance, but that is not intended to be an insult. I'm ignorant of lots of things. Ignorance is something that can be remedied by education."

*

"There are risks in the sheer brevity of Twitter, and it's actually quite an elegant art reducing what you have to say to 140 characters, and it's something that I quite enjoy attempting to do."

*

"I don't feel depressed. I feel elated."

*

"I'm fond of science fiction. But not all science fiction. I like science fiction where there's a scientific lesson, for example - when the science fiction book changes one thing but leaves the rest of science intact and explores the consequences of that. That's actually very valuable."

*

"I don't actually think 'The Selfish Gene' is a very good title. I think that's one of my worst titles."

*

"What's going to happen when I die? I may be buried, or I may be cremated, I may give my body to science. I haven't decided yet."

GORDON FISHER

4 ABOUT OTHER PEOPLE

"How any government could promote the Vardy academies in the North-East of England is absolutely beyond me. Tony Blair defends them on grounds of diversity, but it should be unthinkable in the 21st century to have a school whose head of science believes the world is less than 10,000 years old."

*

"Christopher Hitchens was a great warrior, a magnificent orator, a pugilist and a gentleman. He was kind, but he took no prisoners when arguing with idiots."

*

"It is interesting - you find in the United States, there is a kind of anti-education hostility. It's the sort of Sarah Palin constituency which does seem to actually be hostile to the

New York, Boston, San Francisco educated elite. You
know, 'We good plain folks from the middle of the
country are just as good as you pointy-headed
intellectuals.'"

*

"I think it's misleading to use a word like 'God' in the way
Einstein did. I'm sorry that Einstein did. I think he was
asking for trouble, and he certainly was misunderstood."

*

"The psychologist Elizabeth Loftus has shown great
courage, in the face of spiteful vested interests, in
demonstrating how easy it is for people to concoct
memories that are entirely false but which seem, to the
victim, every bit as real as true memories."

*

"Saddam Hussein could have provided irreplaceable help
to future historians of the Iran/Iraq war, of the invasion of
Kuwait, and of the subsequent era of sanctions
culminating in the current invasion."

*

"If Bush and Blair are eventually put on trial for war

crimes, I shall not be among those pressing for them to be hanged."

*

"The obvious objections to the execution of Saddam Hussein are valid and well aired. His death will provoke violent strife between Sunni and Shia Muslims, and between Iraqis in general and the American occupation forces."

*

"I'm sure Obama is an atheist; I'm sure Kennedy was an atheist, but I doubt if Pope Frank is."

GORDON FISHER

5 GENERAL OPINIONS

"Personally, I rather look forward to a computer program winning the world chess championship. Humanity needs a lesson in humility."

*

"The child has no way of knowing what's good information."

*

"I accept that there may be things far grander and more incomprehensible than we can possibly imagine."

*

"Astrology is an aesthetic affront. It cheapens astronomy, like using Beethoven for commercial jingles."

*

"When you make machines that are capable of obeying instructions slavishly, and among those instructions are 'duplicate me' instructions, then of course the system is wide open to exploitation by parasites."

*

"I am very conscious that you can't condemn people of an earlier era by the standards of ours."

*

"Many people want to send their children to faith schools because they get good exam results, but they're not foolish enough to believe that it's because of faith that they get good exam results."

*

"An Internet meme is a hijacking of the original idea. Instead of mutating by random change and spreading by a form of Darwinian selection, Internet memes are altered deliberately by human creativity. There is no attempt at accuracy of copying, as with genes - and as with memes in their original version."

*

"It is a lamentable observation that because of the way our laws are skewed toward the plaintiff, London has become the libel capital of the world."

*

"To put it bluntly, American political opportunities are heavily loaded against those who are simultaneously intelligent and honest."

*

"I detest 'Jingle Bells,' 'White Christmas,' 'Rudolph the Red Nosed Reindeer,' and the obscene spending bonanza that nowadays seems to occupy not just December, but November and much of October, too."

*

"Why are we so obsessed with monogamous fidelity?"

*

"Teachers who help to open young minds perform a duty which is as near sacred as I will admit."

*

"I do think imagination is enormously valuable, and that children should be encouraged in their imagination. That's very true."

*

"Humans have a proven track record in taking over planes by the use of threats, which work because the legitimate pilots value their own lives and those of their passengers."

*

"A guided missile corrects its trajectory as it flies, homing in, say, on the heat of a jet plane's exhaust. A great improvement on a simple ballistic shell, it still cannot discriminate particular targets. It could not zero in on a designated New York skyscraper if launched from as far away as Boston."

*

"A triumph of consciousness-raising has been the homosexual hijacking of the word 'gay.'"

*

"The population of the U.S. is nearly 300 million, including many of the best educated, most talented, most resourceful, humane people on earth. By almost any measure of civilised attainment, from Nobel prize-counts on down, the U.S. leads the world by miles."

*

"If your plane is being hijacked by an armed man who, though prepared to take risks, presumably wants to go on living, there is room for bargaining."

*

"I think the written word is probably the best medium of communication because you have time to reflect, you have time to choose your words, to get your sentences exactly right. Whereas when you're being interviewed, say, you have to talk on the fly, you have to improvise, you can change sentences around, and they're not exactly right."

*

"What's wrong with being elitist if you are trying to encourage people to join the elite rather than being exclusive?"

*

"We should take astrology seriously. No, I don't mean we should believe in it. I am talking about fighting it seriously instead of humouring it as a piece of harmless fun."

*

"Segregation has no place in the education system."

*

"Anybody who has something sensible or worthwhile to say should be able to say it calmly and soberly, relying on the words themselves to convey his meaning, without resorting to yelling."

*

"I'm afraid the Internet is filled with people using really very intemperate language."

*

"Publishers like a good buzz, and negative responses sell books just as well as positive ones."

*

"Bereavement is terrible, of course. And when somebody you love dies, it's a time for reflection, a time for memory, a time for regret."

*

"We humans are an extremely important manifestation of the replication bomb, because it is through us - through our brains, our symbolic culture and our technology - that the explosion may proceed to the next stage and reverberate through deep space."

*

"If you were to actually travel around schools and universities and listen in on lectures about evolution, you might find a fairly substantial fraction of young people, without knowing what it is they disapprove of, think they disapprove of it, because they've been brought up to."

*

"We are a very, very unusual species."

*

"The reason we personify things like cars and computers is

that just as monkeys live in an arboreal world and moles live in an underground world and water striders live in a surface tension-dominated flatland, we live in a social world."

*

"I think I would abolish schools which systematically inculcate sectarian beliefs."

*

"The enlightenment is under threat. So is reason. So is truth. So is science, especially in the schools of America."

*

"I do understand people when they say that you destroy the magic of childhood if you encourage too much skeptical questioning."

6 GENERAL PHILOSOPHY

"If ever there was a slamming of the door in the face of constructive investigation, it is the word miracle. To a medieval peasant, a radio would have seemed like a miracle."

*

"There is something cheap about magic that works just because it is magic."

*

"We have to find our own purposes in life, which are not derived directly from our scientific history."

*

"I mean I think that when you've got a big brain, when you find yourself planted in a world with a brain big enough to understand quite a lot of what you see around you, but not everything, you naturally fall to thinking about the deep mysteries. Where do we come from? Where does the world come from? Where does the universe come from?"

*

"What is illiberal is not persuasion but imposition of one's views."

*

"How can you take seriously someone who likes to believe something because he finds it 'comforting'?"

*

"You can legally lie about the real world to your heart's content, but until some human being is materially damaged, nobody will complain."

*

"Discrimination is not liberal. Arguing against discrimination is not intolerance."

*

"Natural selection will not remove ignorance from future generations."

*

"A delusion is something that people believe in despite a total lack of evidence."

*

"The universe doesn't owe us condolence or consolation; it doesn't owe us a nice warm feeling inside."

*

"Evil is a miscellaneous collection of nasty things that nasty people do."

*

"The solution often turns out more beautiful than the puzzle."

*

"Isn't it sad to go to your grave without ever wondering why you were born? Who, with such a thought, would not spring from bed, eager to resume discovering the world and rejoicing to be part of it?"

*

"By all means let's be open-minded, but not so open-minded that our brains drop out."

*

"Sometimes I think it's possible to mistake desire for clarity and talking in a no-nonsense way for aggression."

*

"If something is true, no amount of wishful thinking will change it."

*

"The word 'excess' has no meaning for a male."

*

"We admit that we are like apes, but we seldom realise that we are apes."

*

"Let us understand what our own selfish genes are up to because we may then at least have the chance to upset their designs."

*

"Beauty arises out of human inspiration."

*

"I think the world's always a better place if people are filled with understanding."

*

"Design can never be an ultimate explanation for anything. It can only be a proximate explanation. A plane or a car is explained by a designer but that's because the designer himself, the engineer, is explained by natural selection."

*

"If you look up at the Milky Way through the eyes of Carl Sagan, you get a feeling in your chest of something greater than yourself. And it is. But it's not supernatural."

*

"What matters is not the facts but how you discover and think about them."

*

"There may be fairies at the bottom of the garden. There is no evidence for it, but you can't prove that there aren't any, so shouldn't we be agnostic with respect to fairies?"

*

"Intelligent life on a planet comes of age when it first works out the reason for its own existence."

*

"God exists, if only in the form of a meme with high survival value, or infective power, in the environment provided by human culture."

*

"'What is the purpose of the universe?' is a silly question."

*

"Don't kid yourself that you're going to live again after you're dead; you're not. Make the most of the one life you've got. Live it to the full."

*

"A good theory explains a lot but postulates little."

*

"A universe with a creator would be a totally different kind of universe, scientifically speaking, than one without."

*

"The interesting question would be whether there's a Darwinian process, a kind of selection process whereby some memes are more likely to spread than others, because people like them, because they're popular, because they're catchy or whatever it might be."

*

"The chances of each of us coming into existence are infinitesimally small, and even though we shall all die some day, we should count ourselves fantastically lucky to get our decades in the sun."

*

"Let us try to teach generosity and altruism, because we are born selfish."

7 ON RELIGION

"You can't understand European history at all other than through religion, or English literature either if you can't recognise biblical allusions."

*

"I am against religion because it teaches us to be satisfied with not understanding the world."

*

"I suppose I'm a cultural Anglican, and I see evensong in a country church through much the same eyes as I see a village cricket match on the village green. I have a certain love for it."

*

"People believe the only alternative to randomness is intelligent design."

*

"I once wrote that anybody who believes the world is only 6,000 years old is either ignorant, stupid, insane or wicked."

*

"One of the things that is wrong with religion is that it teaches us to be satisfied with answers which are not really answers at all."

*

"The very idea that we get a moral compass from religion is horrible. Not only should we not get our moral compass from religion, as a matter of fact we don't."

*

"There are many very educated people who are religious, but they're not creationists."

*

"Presumably what happened to Jesus was what happens to all of us when we die. We decompose. Accounts of Jesus's resurrection and ascension are about as well-documented as Jack and the Beanstalk."

*

"Many of us saw religion as harmless nonsense. Beliefs might lack all supporting evidence but, we thought, if people needed a crutch for consolation, where's the harm? September 11th changed all that."

*

"God stands out in the universe as the most glaring of all superfluous sore thumbs."

*

"What has 'theology' ever said that is of the smallest use to anybody? When has 'theology' ever said anything that is demonstrably true and is not obvious? What makes you think that 'theology' is a subject at all?"

*

"Do you advocate the Ten Commandments as a guide to the good life? Then I can only presume that you don't know the Ten Commandments."

*

"In Britain, Christianity is dying. Islam, unfortunately, isn't."

*

"The question of whether there exists a supernatural creator, a God, is one of the most important that we have to answer. I think that it is a scientific question. My answer is no."

*

"Religion teaches you to be satisfied with nonanswers. It's a sort of crime against childhood."

*

"If saying that religion should be a private matter and should not have special influence in public life is illiberal, then 74% of U.K. Christians are illiberal, too."

*

"The very idea of supernatural magic - including miracles - is incoherent, devoid of sensible meaning."

*

"We've all been brought up with the view that religion has some kind of special privileged status. You're not allowed to criticise it."

*

"Even if you believe a creator god invented the laws of physics, would you so insult him as to suggest that he might capriciously and arbitrarily violate them in order to walk on water, or turn water into wine as a cheap party trick at a wedding?"

*

"Religion is about turning untested belief into unshakable truth through the power of institutions and the passage of time."

*

GORDON FISHER

"There are many religious points of view where the conservation of the world is just as important as it is to scientists."

*

"The idea of an afterlife where you can be reunited with loved ones can be immensely consoling - though not to me."

*

"It has become almost a cliche to remark that nobody boasts of ignorance of literature, but it is socially acceptable to boast ignorance of science and proudly claim incompetence in mathematics."

*

"The meme for blind faith secures its own perpetuation by the simple unconscious expedient of discouraging rational inquiry."

*

"It's a horrible idea that God, this paragon of wisdom and knowledge, power, couldn't think of a better way to forgive us our sins than to come down to Earth in his alter ego as his son and have himself hideously tortured and executed so that he could forgive himself."

*

"I am baffled by the way sophisticated theologians who know Adam and Eve never existed still keep talking about it."

*

"Nothing is wrong with peace and love. It is all the more regrettable that so many of Christ's followers seem to disagree."

*

"The Bible was written by fallible human beings."

*

"Secularism is categorically not saying that the religious may not speak out publicly or have a say in public life. It is about saying that religion alone should not confer a privileged say in public life, or greater influence on it. It really is as simple as that."

*

"All the great religions have a place for awe, for ecstatic transport at the wonder and beauty of creation."

*

"In the World Wars, people were perfectly able to shoot other people just because they belonged to the wrong country, without ever asking what their opinions were. Faith too is like that."

*

"If we are too friendly to nice, decent bishops, we run the risk of buying into the fiction that there's something virtuous about believing things because of faith rather than because of evidence. We run the risk of betraying scientific enlightenment."

*

"It would be intolerant if I advocated the banning of religion, but of course I never have."

*

"At least the fundamentalists haven't tried to dilute their message. Their faith is exposed for what it is for all to see."

*

"Faith is the great cop-out, the great excuse to evade the need to think and evaluate evidence. Faith is belief in spite of, even perhaps because of, the lack of evidence."

*

"I think my love of truth and honesty forces me to notice that the liberal intelligentsia of Western countries is betraying itself where Islam is concerned."

*

"The earliest books in the New Testament to be written were the Epistles, not the Gospels. It's almost as though Saint Paul and others who wrote the Epistles weren't that interested in whether Jesus was real."

*

"I get the feeling more and more that religion is being left behind."

*

"I do feel visceral revulsion at the burka because for me it is a symbol of the oppression of women."

*

"A native speaker of English who has never read a word of the King James Bible is verging on the barbarian."

*

"Notoriously, the United States is the most religious of the Western advanced nations. It's a bit mysterious why that is."

*

"I do disapprove very strongly of labelling children, especially young children, as something like 'Catholic children' or 'Protestant children' or 'Islamic children.'"

*

"Religion is capable of driving people to such dangerous folly that faith seems to me to qualify as a kind of mental illness."

*

"The whole idea of creating saints, it's pure 'Monty Python.' They have to clock up two miracles."

*

"We cannot, of course, disprove God, just as we can't disprove Thor, fairies, leprechauns and the Flying Spaghetti Monster."

*

"People really, really hate their religion being criticized. It's as though you've said they had an ugly face; they seem to identify personally with it."

*

"Religious organisations have an automatic tax-free charitable status."

*

"Something about the cultural tradition of Jews is way, way more sympathetic to science and learning and intellectual pursuits than Islam."

*

"Religious fanatics want people to switch off their own minds, ignore the evidence, and blindly follow a holy book based upon private 'revelation'."

*

"The Bible should be taught, but emphatically not as reality. It is fiction, myth, poetry, anything but reality. As such it needs to be taught because it underlies so much of our literature and our culture."

*

"A universe with a God would look quite different from a universe without one. A physics, a biology where there is a God is bound to look different. So the most basic claims of religion are scientific. Religion is a scientific theory."

*

"I think a fundamentalist is somebody who believes something unshakably and isn't going to change their mind."

*

"If there is a God, it's going to be a whole lot bigger and a whole lot more incomprehensible than anything that any theologian of any religion has ever proposed."

8 ON SCIENCE

"Scientists disagree among themselves but they never fight over their disagreements. They argue about evidence or go out and seek new evidence. Much the same is true of philosophers, historians and literary critics."

*

"My eyes are constantly wide open to the extraordinary fact of existence. Not just human existence, but the existence of life and how this breathtakingly powerful process, which is natural selection, has managed to take the very simple facts of physics and chemistry and build them up to redwood trees and humans."

*

"Far from being demeaning to human spiritual values, scientific rationalism is the crowning glory of the human spirit."

*

"All the fossils that we have ever found have always been found in the appropriate place in the time sequence. There are no fossils in the wrong place."

*

"We are a unique ape. We have language. Other animals have systems of communication that fall far short of that. They don't have the same ability to communicate complicated conditionals and what-ifs and talk about things that are not present."

*

"Evolution never looks to the future."

*

"It is possible in medicine, even when you intend to do good, to do harm instead. That is why science thrives on actively encouraging criticism rather than stifling it."

*

"A good scientific theory is one which is falsifiable, which has not been falsified."

*

"But perhaps the rest of us could have separate classes in science appreciation, the wonder of science, scientific ways of thinking, and the history of scientific ideas, rather than laboratory experience."

*

"Something pretty mysterious had to give rise to the origin of the universe."

*

"I am one of those scientists who feels that it is no longer enough just to get on and do science. We have to devote a significant proportion of our time and resources to defending it from deliberate attack from organised ignorance."

*

"There's clearly a lot of Ludditism, and you see it in all the hysteria about every scientific story."

*

"Of course you can use the products of science to do bad things, but you can use them to do good things, too."

*

"Science, as opposed to technology, does violence to common sense."

*

"A constellation is not an entity at all, not the kind of thing that Uranus, or anything else, can sensibly be said to 'move into.'"

*

"From a Darwinian perspective, it is clear what pain is doing. It's a warning: 'Don't do that again.' If you burn yourself, you're never going to pick up a live coal again."

*

"You can't even begin to understand biology, you can't understand life, unless you understand what it's all there for, how it arose - and that means evolution."

*

"Today the theory of evolution is about as much open to doubt as the theory that the earth goes round the sun."

*

"I have a strong feeling that the subject of evolution is beautiful without the excuse of creationists needing to be bashed."

*

"What Darwinian theory shows us is that all human races are extremely close to each other. None of them is in any sense ancestral to any other; none of them is more primitive than any other. We are all modern races of exactly equal status, evolutionarily speaking."

*

"Of course in science there are things that are open to doubt and things need to be discussed. But among the things that science does know, evolution is about as certain as anything we know."

*

"It's very likely that most mammals have consciousness, and probably birds, too."

*

"For the first half of geological time our ancestors were bacteria. Most creatures still are bacteria, and each one of our trillions of cells is a colony of bacteria."

*

"Any teaching of falsehoods in science classes should certainly be identified and stopped by school inspectors. School inspectors should be looking at science teachings to make sure they are evidence-based science."

*

"If you set out in a spaceship to find the one planet in the galaxy that has life, the odds against your finding it would be so great that the task would be indistinguishable, in practice, from impossible."

*

"The fact that life evolved out of nearly nothing, some 10 billion years after the universe evolved out of literally nothing, is a fact so staggering that I would be mad to attempt words to do it justice."

*

"For me, the level at which natural selection causes the phenomenon of adaptation is the level of the replicator - the gene."

*

"I am very comfortable with the idea that we can override biology with free will."

*

"Islands are natural workshops of evolution."

*

"Public sharing is an important part of science."

*

"I'm fascinated by the idea that genetics is digital. A gene is a long sequence of coded letters, like computer information. Modern biology is becoming very much a branch of information technology."

*

"Natural selection is anything but random."

*

"Physicists are working on the Big Bang, and one day they may or may not solve it."

*

"The theory of evolution by cumulative natural selection is the only theory we know of that is in principle capable of explaining the existence of organized complexity."

*

"Selfish genes actually explain altruistic individuals, and to me that's crystal-clear."

*

"The very large brain that humans have, plus the things that go along with it - language, art, science - seemed to have evolved only once. The eye, by contrast, independently evolved 40 times. So, if you were to 'replay' evolution, the eye would almost certainly appear again, whereas the big brain probably wouldn't."

*

"I'm pretty sure there is some genetic component towards intelligence."

*

"At the deepest level, all living things that have ever been looked at have the same DNA code. And many of the same genes."

*

"Science coverage could be improved by the recognition that science is timeless, and therefore science stories should not need to be pegged to an item in the news."

*

"The world is well supplied with spiders whose male ancestors died after mating. The world is bereft of spiders whose would-be ancestors never mated in the first place."

*

"There does seem to be a sense in which physics has gone beyond what human intuition can understand. We shouldn't be too surprised about that because we're evolved to understand things that move at a medium pace at a medium scale. We can't cope with the very tiny scale of quantum physics or the very large scale of relativity."

*

"Even if 'going retrograde' or 'moving into Aquarius' were real phenomena, something that planets actually do, what influence could they possibly have on human events? A planet is so far away that its gravitational pull on a newborn baby would be swamped by the gravitational pull of the doctor's paunch."

*

"In the 1920s and 1930s, scientists from both the political left and right would not have found the idea of designer babies particularly dangerous - though, of course, they would not have used that phrase."

*

"It's an important point to realize that the genetic programming of our lives is not fully deterministic. It is statistical - it is in any animal merely statistical - not deterministic."

*

"I would like people to appreciate science in the same way they appreciate the arts."

*

"Science has taught us, against all intuition, that apparently solid things like crystals and rocks are really almost entirely composed of empty space. And the familiar illustration is the nucleus of an atom is a fly in the middle of a sports stadium, and the next atom is in the next sports stadium."

*

"Every night of our lives, we dream, and our brain concocts visions which are, at least until we wake up, highly convincing. Most of us have had experiences which are verging on hallucination. It shows the power of the brain to knock up illusions."

*

"Our animal origins are constantly lurking behind, even if

they are filtered through complicated social evolution."

*

"There's branches of science which I don't understand; for example, physics. It could be said, I suppose, that I have faith that physicists understand it better than I do."

*

"Science - or the products of science like technology - is just a way of achieving something real, something that happens, something that works."

*

"Biology is the study of complicated things that have the appearance of having been designed with a purpose."

*

"Mystics exult in mystery and want it to stay mysterious. Scientists exult in mystery for a different reason: It gives them something to do."

*

"There is no refutation of Darwinian evolution in existence. If a refutation ever were to come about, it would come from a scientist, and not an idiot."

*

"The essence of life is statistical improbability on a colossal scale."

*

"Placebos work."

*

"Why did humans lose their body hair? Why did they start walking on their hind legs? Why did they develop big brains? I think that the answer to all three questions is sexual selection."

THE VERY BEST OF RICHARD DAWKINS

Printed in Great Britain
by Amazon.co.uk, Ltd.,
Marston Gate.